Copyright © 1996 by Michael Neugebauer Verlag AG, Gossau Zürich, Switzerland.
First published in Switzerland under the title DAS WÜSTENFUCHS KINDER-BUCH
English translation copyright © 1996 by North-South Books Inc.

All rights reserved. No part of this book may be reproduced or utilized in any form or
by any means, electronic or mechanical, including photocopying, recording, or any
information storage and retrieval system, without permission in writing from the publisher.

First published in the United States, Canada, Great Britain, Australia, and New Zealand in 1996
by North-South Books, an imprint of Nord-Süd Verlag AG, Gossau Zürich, Switzerland.

Distributed in the United States by North-South Books Inc., New York.

Library of Congress Cataloging-in-Publication Data is available.
A CIP catalogue record for this book is available from The British Library.
ISBN 1-55858-579-6 (trade binding) 10 9 8 7 6 5 4 3 2 1
ISBN 1-55858-580-X (library binding) 10 9 8 7 6 5 4 3 2 1
Printed in Italy

Ask your bookseller for these other North-South Animal Family Books:
THE CROCODILE FAMILY BOOK by Mark Deeble and Victoria Stone
THE GRIZZLY BEAR FAMILY BOOK by Michio Hoshino
THE LION FAMILY BOOK by Angelika Hofer and Gunter Ziesler
THE PENGUIN FAMILY BOOK by Lauritz Somme and Sybille Kalas
THE ELEPHANT FAMILY BOOK by Oria Douglas-Hamilton

The Desert Fox Family Book

Hans Gerold Laukel

Translated by Rosemary Lanning

A MICHAEL NEUGEBAUER BOOK / NORTH-SOUTH BOOKS / NEW YORK / LONDON

I was on my very first school outing, a visit to the Frankfurt Zoo, and all around me were animals, from the huge elephant to the tiny leaf-cutting ant. I was only ten years old and had seen very few of these animals before. They made a deep impression on me.

Among all these unfamiliar creatures was one small animal that enchanted me from the moment I saw it. It had soft, sandy fur and a bushy tail, like a fox's. From a sweet, mischievous face, black button eyes gazed fixedly at me, seeming to size me up. But its huge bat ears fascinated me most of all. On the information plate I read:

FENNEC, or DESERT FOX (Fennecus zerda)

Habitat: sandy deserts from North Africa to the Middle East.

Secretive, nocturnal.

From that moment I dreamed of visiting this little imp with the big ears in its own home one day.

Now, many years later, my dream has come true. I am in North Africa, in the Sahara, the world's largest desert. By day it is so hot here that you could fry eggs on the rocks, but at night the temperature falls below 32 degrees Fahrenheit (0 degrees centigrade). Only a small part of the Sahara is as I had imagined it, an endless sea of sand dunes. Most of it is a vast plain, with rugged black rocks, and riverbeds that dried up long ago. There are trees, flowers, birds, and even fish here, and with luck I may also find my little friend the fennec.

Ever since I arrived here a sandstorm has been sweeping through the wadi—the dried-up riverbed—with unbelievable force. All day and all night sharp grains of sand rattle against my small tent. Finer grains blow in through ventilation holes and seams. Every inch of my equipment, even my camera, is covered in sandy dust.

I'm worried about how much longer this bad weather will last. I had planned to camp in this hollow between the dunes for a month or more, watching and photographing fennecs. But if the storm keeps up, I can't possibly stay.

Then, suddenly, in the morning, the nightmare is over. The weather has changed without warning. The sun is shining again, out of a radiantly blue sky. The air is clear and dry. I creep carefully along the sheer side of the wadi to my observation post on the highest rocky ledge. From here I have a good view over the valley through which the riverbed runs. A vast expanse of dunes stretches out in front of me, and at the end of the valley the Ksar Oasis, with its green date palms and two white minarets, rises out of the yellow sea of sand.

This is where my friends, the Bedouin, live. These desert people love fennecs as much as I do, and I have learned a lot from them about the animals' way of life. Sometimes they keep fennecs as pets, to protect their houses from snakes and scorpions, and to bring them luck. They have helped me find "my" fennecs, a pair that raise their cubs here in the wadi every spring. Courtship and mating take place between January and March. After 50 days the mother gives birth to 2 to 4 young. The cubs open their eyes after about two weeks. At this age they begin to take solid food in addition to their mother's milk.

The fennec is the smallest of all the wild dogs, only 8 inches (20 cm) tall at the shoulders and weighing about 3 pounds (1.5 kg). It is very well suited to its environment. The soles of the fennec's feet are thickly covered in fur, to help it move silently across the dunes and not sink into the sand. To stop its temperature from rising too high, it follows a strict timetable, foraging for food only at night or in the cooler morning hours. The rest of the day the fennec spends underground in its burrow.

Of all predators, the fennec has by far the largest ears in proportion to its body. These ears may measure up to 6 inches (15 cm). With them it can pick up the smallest sounds, even from under the desert sand. Its diet, in addition to various insects, consists mainly of jerboas and other rodents, snakes, lizards, scorpions, birds, fruit, and plants. When hunting very small prey such as insects, its ears point forward like satellite dishes to detect the slightest movement. But the desert fox's ears also serve another purpose: They help to regulate its body temperature. Fennecs, like dogs, have no sweat glands. They keep cool by panting, and by using the cooling system in their ears. Blood flowing through vessels near the surface of the ears is cooled by air movement.

My fennec cubs are now four weeks old. Every day, and on many a cold night, I watch them from my tent or my observation post on the rocks. The fennec family's burrow is only a few yards (meters) from my small camouflaged tent, in a mound of sand topped by a big tuft of grass. The burrow has three entrances. The larger, main entrance leads into the root system under the grass. The two other, much narrower tunnels come out at the foot of the mound. The fennecs' living quarters lie deep in the middle of the sandy mound, amid the grass roots. All the tunnels end there. In the area outside the tunnels I have found the fennec cubs' toys: root fragments, gaudy feathers, bones, small stones, and scraps of fur.

Every morning, when the first warm rays of sunshine strike the entrance of the burrow, the young fennecs come out into the open. One small black nose after another pushes out of the hole. Watchful and alert, the cubs sniff the still, cool morning air all around. Only when they are sure that the coast is clear, that there are no birds of prey hovering overhead and no other enemies, such as hyenas or jackals, close by, do they come all the way out. At first they stay under the cover of the overhanging grass. Then, suddenly, nothing can hold them back. One of the cubs dashes out and races around the sandy mound. A second cub follows, then a third and a fourth, and a wild chase begins, in and out and all around the clump of grass.

Two of the little fennecs square up to each other with their mouths wide open, wagging their short, glossy tails. It is only a play fight. They tumble over each other, squeaking, scuffling, and turning somersaults down the slope. The two other cubs play at stalking. First they hide, and then they hurtle through the long, rustling grass in clumsy leaps. When they have tired themselves out, they snuggle together in the warm sand in front of the burrow. They are enjoying their rest. They yawn and stretch and loll about in the warm morning sun.

The cubs doze for quite a while, until a strange noise makes all four heads pop up at once. The young fennecs gaze fixedly at the far side of the wadi.
A Bedouin from the oasis village is leading his camels through the valley. He has been collecting the fresh spring grass that grows luxuriantly after the winter rain, and will use it to feed his sheep and goats.

Heavily laden with huge bundles of hay, the caravan moves slowly towards the village. But to the fennec cubs, these large animals with their enormous burdens look frightening. All at once the cubs are gone, hurrying to safety inside their burrow.

The only traces of the fennec cubs' abandoned game are the hundreds of tiny footprints in the sand. The cubs will now spend the hottest hours of the day in the cool burrow.

Outside in the valley the sun climbs higher into the blue, cloudless sky and heats the dark cliffs of the wadi, making them as hot as an oven. Last winter's rains turned the river into a raging torrent. A tidemark of palm-tree trunks, roots, grass, and stones still shows the force of the wild brown water in its flood.

By now, in early April, the last puddles are quickly evaporating. In the heat of the sun a wafer-thin crust forms on top of the mud. Then it splits open, forming strange and striking patterns. Seeds of desert plants are trapped in the cracks and crevices. Very soon countless small islands of green appear on the dry riverbed.

For years the seeds of grasses and flowers slumbered in the desert sand. After last winter's rains they all awoke, as if at a secret signal, to unfold their delicate green leaves and beautiful flowers. By mid May they must all have set seed, for by then the heat will be so intense that even the hardiest plants will shrivel.

In the Saharan spring, the desert is alive with activity. Birds called bee eaters are nesting in tunnels, and for thorn-tailed lizards, skinks, snakes, and jerboas this is also the best time to breed. Small rodents called gundis scurry through cracks in the stony walls of the riverbank. They are rearing young too and are especially watchful. A few migratory birds that overwintered in the Sahara are still moving north. Some of them, such as swallows, hoopoes, and bee eaters, land in the wadi, exhausted after their strenuous flight across the desert. They need to rest, but must be on guard against the hungry mother fennec.

Desert animals can usually find as much food as they need. Fennecs will drink water when it's available, but they are able to survive for long periods with minimum intake of fluids. They dig for roots—a valuable source of water—and eat insects, rodents, birds, and eggs. The mother fennec has to go hunting frequently. She prefers to wait until after sunset, but sometimes, if the cubs are hungry, she will go out when the sun is high, to catch something for them and bring it back to the burrow. Today I see her out and about late in the afternoon. She leaves the burrow by the back entrance and walks towards the wadi. From my position on the cliffs I can track her easily with my field glasses. She runs along the riverbed with her ears pricked, stopping beside each tuft of grass to examine it thoroughly.

Now and then she pounces on a fat black beetle, throws it in the air, catches it in her mouth, crunches it and swallows it hastily. She stops by a large stone. Something behind it seems to interest her.

She creeps around the stone, then suddenly stands rooted to the spot—face to face with the large green thorn-tailed lizard that had been basking there. The lizard opens its mouth wide in threat and whips its tail. The mother fennec backs off, and continues her hunt further along the valley.

Soon afterward she finds a small, venomous sand viper. The snake writhes and rattles its scales to scare the desert fox. But she simply trots away.

She rounds a corner of the wadi and stops beside a scrubby bush. She crawls carefully through its overhanging branches, right into the middle. Suddenly there is a loud hissing and rustling. The whole bush shudders. The mother fennec has tracked down a desert monitor. Like the thorn-tailed lizard, it keeps the hungry fox at bay by whipping its tail from side to side, and it spits and hisses ferociously, opening its mouth wide. The fennec won't try to attack it. It is much too large for her.

The mother fennec turns away from the hostile creature in the bush and lopes across to the yellow dunes. There she probes the warm sand with her pointed muzzle, chasing skinks, a species of lizard. Skinks can burrow and move through the sand at tremendous speed, almost as if they are swimming. That's why the Bedouin call them sand fish.

Suddenly the fennec pounces like a cat catching a mouse, and clasps a wriggling silver skink in her mouth. But she does not eat her catch. She kills the skink and then buries it in the loose sand of the dune, and goes on hunting. When she has hidden four or five sand fish in various places, she carefully collects all the dead skinks and runs quickly along the wadi to bring her plentiful catch home to her cubs.

The sun has sunk behind the chain of dunes and the air is now dusky and cool. The fennec cubs have emerged from their burrow. They lie close together, well hidden under the greenish-grey tussock of grass. They are very hungry, and watch the riverbed attentively for their mother's return.

The mother fennec does not go straight to the burrow. She waits quite a while at a safe distance, between the rocks at the edge of the wadi. She has to be sure that she is not being watched as she approaches her cubs, because the golden jackal, which preys on fennecs, has its own hunting grounds in the wadi and prowls through the valley every evening. Only when the mother fennec is sure that no danger threatens does she approach her burrow.

The cubs have seen her coming from a long way off. They crawl underneath her, whimpering and cowering. She opens her mouth, and each of the cubs seizes a fat sand fish. They gulp down the food greedily. When siblings come too close together, they snarl furiously and push each other with their hind-quarters. Sometimes fierce fights break out.

All is quiet outside the desert foxes' burrow. Each of the cubs has eaten its share of the food. Tired and satisfied, the family goes back into the burrow. During the night the mother fox will go hunting again.

In early May the Saharan spring is nearing its end. Summer brings great heat to the valley, and all the puddles have dried up. The first of the desert plants shed their seeds.

My young fennecs are now two months old. They have extended their playground wider and wider. Sometimes their mother takes them with her as far as the rocks in the valley.

Today is a special day for the whole family. Father fennec has come on a visit. They have seen him only rarely over the past weeks. He has crept up to the burrow now and then, but secretly and always at night. While I have never seen him bring anything for the cubs to eat, male fennecs do help provide food for their families. The cubs behave quite differently this morning. Instead of romping in their usual exuberant way, they crawl around their father, whimpering submissively.

Father fennec devotes himself to each of the cubs in turn, licking its face and ears. Mother fennec stretches out in a hollow in the sand. The cubs keep urging her to play, and they jump on her roughly. But the female fox is tired after her nocturnal hunt. She pushes the cubs away, curls up, and goes to sleep.

Sadness is creeping over me. The cubs are growing so quickly. I suspect that the mother fennec will soon lead them over to the cliffs—maybe even today. She will take her children with her more and more often, on longer and longer hunting trips. The cubs will try to trap the nimble gundis or catch locusts. They will learn how to deal with poisonous snakes and other hazards. Their mother will show them where the fattest sand fish are, and how to get hold of the sweet, ripe dates in the oasis gardens in autumn. Soon the cubs will be so big and strong that it will be hard to tell them from their parents. At one year, they will be fully mature. Then they will go their own ways. Next winter, when the weather is coolest and sandstorms rage through the desert, the fennecs will mate. And I hope that when the desert spring returns, four more young scalawags with big ears will come and play in front of their burrow beneath the tussock of grass, here in the Sahara.

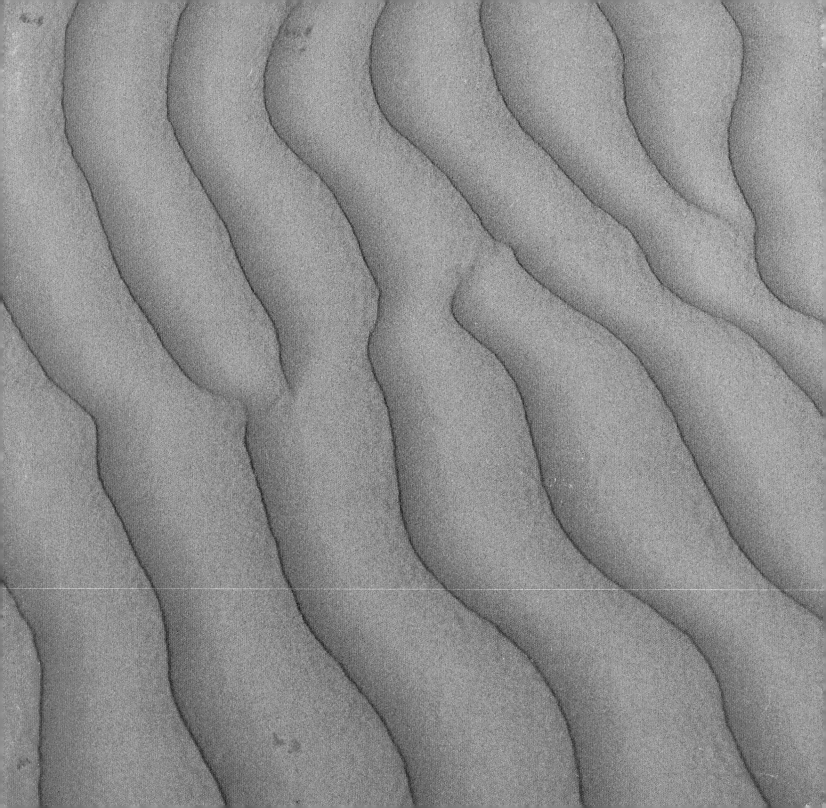